PRINCIPLES
IN MAINTAINING
A GODLY
ORGANIZATION

K.P. YOHANNAN

BOOKS

a division of Gospel for Asia

www.gfa.org

Principles in Maintaining a Godly Organization

© 2003 by K.P. Yohannan

All Scripture quotations, unless otherwise indicated, are
taken from the New King James Version. Copyright ©
1982 by Thomas Nelson, Inc. Used by permission.
All rights reserved.

Scripture quotations marked KJV are taken from the King
James Version Bible. Public Domain.

ISBN: 978-1-59589-008-5

Published by gfa books, a division of Gospel for Asia
1800 Golden Trail Court, Carrollton, TX 75010 USA
phone: (972) 300-7777
fax: (972) 300-7778

Printed in the United States of America

For information about other materials, visit our website:
www.gfa.org.

11 12 13 14 15 / 8 7 6 5

To my son, Daniel. I am deeply grateful to the Lord for your servant-hearted leadership. I am proud of you.

Table of Contents

Introduction

————◆◆◆————

When we look back at the history of church movements and Christian organizations, we often find they began with great dreams and ambitions. The leadership was strong and on fire for God—and then somehow, something went wrong. The life went out of them. They became "just another organization." Study the beginning years of some of the major denominations and see how red-hot they were. Look at them now and see where they are! You are in for a shock!

I have seen this trend too often in Christian ministry, where things go well for so long, tremendous progress is made, the Lord's kingdom is going forward—but then, over time, things start heading downhill.

This is a great concern to me as I think about the movement of which I am a part. It is my prayer that the Lord will help us continue on course, that we will stay focused and not lose the original vision He gave us, and that we will maintain our vibrancy and joy over the great possibilities He is laying before us.

That is why I believe it is good for us to continually go back to the Scriptures, rather than to the philosophies and structures created by human experts on building great organizations. From Scripture we can see how God called people and empowered them, how they succeeded, how they failed and how they returned to the Lord after their failures. We can learn valuable and vital lessons from their lives. As Paul says in 1 Corinthians 10:11, "Now all these things happened to them as examples, and they were written for our admonition."

One powerful example we have is the early Church in the book of Acts. You see a fresh beginning, leading and newness. You see excitement and unity and togetherness. You see a cause to live and die for. If we can understand the hearts of these believers more deeply, grasp the principles that worked in their everyday lives and made them what they were, and then adjust ourselves accordingly, I believe this will help us more than we can ever realize.

Because each one of us is an individual, it is not always easy to think of our part in the organization in terms of this bigger picture. By default we think about the immediate—the experience we are going through right now. It takes a good deal of maturity, understanding from the Lord and deliberate thinking to put ourselves in the context of the world in which we live today, realizing that our lives are short and what we do now can truly impact eternity. Jesus told us that the road to eternal life was narrow, and few would find it (Matthew 7:14); and unless we make it a point to think about ourselves as the Lord does, we can easily miss the significance of our call.

What I share in this booklet I have learned over the past couple decades of experience with Gospel for Asia. I pray that you will take the time to think deeply about what you will be reading and learning. Let your understanding and response go beyond your intellect or your emotions.

CHAPTER ONE

How It Begins

———◆———

If you look at any movement that God begins, you will see three distinct characteristics. You will find these in the early Church.

Let us take some time and go back to the book of Acts, to the very beginnings of the Church. If we can live with these believers for a while and feel what they felt, I believe we can return to our own situations and circumstances with some timeless principles.

It Is Radical

It does not take long when reading through Acts to discover that these believers were radical—they were willing to take all kinds of risks. To the rest of the world they were crazy people, blind to reality—nuts!

But this is what Jesus was after—radical, fearless men and women. These were the kinds of people He was looking for when He told them:

> But you shall receive power when the Holy Spirit has come upon you; and you shall be witnesses to Me in Jerusalem, and in all Judea and Samaria, and to the end of the earth (Acts 1:8).

When the early Christians understood that Christ had risen, victorious over sin and death, they readily burned all their bridges behind them and said, in essence, "There's nothing to go back to. This is a one-way trip" (see Acts 2:45; 4:19–20; 5:29–32; 7:51–60).

At this time in history, the city of Jerusalem was completely anti-Christian. Imagine trying to preach the Gospel out in the open today in the nation of Afghanistan or in a Hindu temple—believe me, that would be easier than doing so in Jerusalem in A.D. 33. The early Christians knew they would be beaten up and put in prison if they preached the Gospel (see Acts 8:3). It did not matter to them—they did it anyway, considering it an honor to suffer for Christ's sake (Acts 5:41).

These people were so radical that nothing would stop them. They were not concerned with preserving their lives. They were bold and adventurous. They were open to new ideas. They wouldn't take "no" for an answer. They were motivated from within rather than from tradition. They were willing to endure any hardship, but they wouldn't keep their mouths shut. And ultimately these characteristics earned them the reputation of being "world revolutionaries" (see Acts 17:6).

When I think back to the beginnings of our movement, I see that same radical attitude in our early days. I can honestly tell you, I don't know how on earth we did what we did! The way so many of our programs developed was not through planning, scheming or figuring. They just happened out of spontaneity, love, dreams, hopes and ambitions rather than out of rules or regulations. We were not on any kind of schedule or timetable. Today I carry a planner with me to help me remember my appointments—but I had nothing of the sort then. I did not know just what was going to happen, but it did—amazingly and radically so.

It Is Transformational

The people involved in the tremendous growth of the early Church were not considered to be tools used to get things done. Rather, they threw their lives into their calling, and all the while God was using them to impact the world and carry out His plan, they themselves were actually being continually transformed and changed in the process.

Jesus focused on people's potential instead of on weakness. He did not recruit perfect people, but people who could change, who would have a heart commitment. You've read enough of the Gospels to know that His disciples came from the dregs of society. (Gayle Erwin talks about this in detail in *The Jesus Style*.[1]) Just imagine the scenario that surrounded Jesus in just the last 48 hours of His life: 12 men fighting among themselves over who was greatest . . . one of His closest followers betraying Him . . . and the rest running away when the danger got too close. Yet He entrusted these men, in whom He had invested three years of His life, to carry on the calling God had given Him. It was unto Peter, who denied His Master three times, that Jesus gave the keys of the kingdom (see Matthew 26:75; 16:18–19)!

Think about the apostle Paul after he met Jesus on the road to Damascus. Most believers did not want to have anything to do with him. "He's dangerous," they believed (see Acts 9:21, 26). But then you see Barnabas enter the scene, put his arm around Paul and vouch for his integrity to the early Church (Acts 9:27). And Paul, who had once worked tirelessly to persecute believers in Jesus and eradicate all traces of Christianity, becomes totally transformed into one of the greatest apostles who ever lived. How did this happen? Not all in one day, but in a process that took time, starting with 14 years out in the wilderness.

In our early days, when we thought about recruiting staff members, we had no application form or interview process. I'll never forget the day when one couple just showed up on our doorstep with their little baby in their arms, ready to serve God with us. I never even thought to ask him for references! It was all so fresh and amazing.

You'll find that same wonder, awe and fear of God in the beginnings of any organization. God just brings people—no forms to be filled out—He works in their lives and changes them, and then uses them to change others. It is a continuous, perpetual motion in which somehow things just keep happening. Nobody stops to think about how!

You see, God is always more concerned about people than about what they can do. And if we follow Him, He will make sure that we keep this in mind. God's approach is always from the inside out (Luke 11:39–40;

Psalm 51:6). Character is the important thing. If this is taken care of, the rest will follow.

Jesus' only requirement for those who wanted to be His disciples was that they obey and follow (Matthew 16:24). He did not ask about anything else. He knew, like a potter, that if the clay would submit, He could mold and transform it to become the most precious vessel to be used for His kingdom.

It Is Relational

The third characteristic that marks the beginning of any movement of God is that everything happens through relationship, just as we see in the book of Acts (Acts 2:42, 44–47).

When Jesus sent the disciples out to the villages, He sent them two by two, not one by one (Luke 10:1). If you look in the Gospel of John, beginning with chapter 13, Jesus gives His disciples some final instructions before He goes to the cross. But the crux of His message has nothing to do with world evangelism, changing the world, the reality of hell, how to start an organization or a list of rules. All He simply said was, "If you love one another, the world will know you are My disciples." His prayers, His concern had everything to do with this one truth.

And how did Paul do his work? Read his epistles, and you will find such phrases as these: "This brother greets you," or "this sister greets you," or "the church in your house . . . (see Romans 16:23, 1 Corinthians 16:19, Colossians 4:15). And at the end of each letter there always seems to be a list of names tagged on. You will always find relationships working here. Paul's life and ministry have everything to do with working with others.

We are commanded to forgive one another, to bear one another's burdens. Look at Romans 12 and Philippians 2, as well as other Scripture portions that deal with our relationship toward one another in the Body of Christ. You will see clearly that this is how God works. This is His plan to get things done.

As time passes, unfortunately, these three natural distinctives that mark a fresh movement of God will naturally degrade. Let us look at these changes in the next chapter.

CHAPTER TWO

What Happened?

———◆•◆———

Someone once said that within the timeline of any movement, the original life, passion and vision would be sustained about 25 years. The excitement, freshness and newness are on a basic uphill incline up to that point. After that, things will begin to change. There will be more of a plateau effect on the distinctives of the movement.

During the early days of my ministry with Operation Mobilization, I heard its founder, George Verwer, speak about the problem of losing vision and passion. He said, "God raises up a man with a vision and heart for God, and that becomes a movement. Then it turns into a machine. Then it ends up becoming a monument, and it is history. It is dead."

This is exactly what happened to the YMCA, the Salvation Army and most mainline denominations, such as Methodist, Lutheran and Moravian. What glorious beginnings they had under godly leaders! But now look at some of the mission organizations of the past and see—where are they today? The vision, the burden and passion are gone.

Unfortunately, I have found this to be true in organizations I have known. But the greater question to ask is when will we ever learn from the failure of others? Let us take a look at what changes.

Radical Becomes Conventional

In the secular world, a business's generation is also said to last about 25 years, after which freshness and vision—and thus success—decline. Japanese organizations, however, have manipulated this time frame through education and structure changes. They begin to implement changes after only about 10 years, before people become set in their ways and find difficulty adapting to change. In this way, businesses are perpetually moving on, without losing their edge and success in the industry.

After a certain point in the life of a movement, things somehow shift into "maintenance" mode. The life that was once radical is now a part of the past, a part of history; now the goal is simply to "do it the way we've always done it." What was once a fresh, flexible way of doing things now becomes a hard, stiff structure of rules, regulations and bylaws that we build around ourselves to feel some sort of protection.

Individuals now have positions on a variety of levels—some you can approach directly and others you cannot. By the time you attempt to go where you want within the organization, the structure is so complex you almost need a road map to navigate the maze!

A movement that has gone from radical to conventional is no longer regulated by vision and faith; instead, the decisions that come out of it are based on careful calculations of the lowest risk possible. Prayer meetings become planning meetings. Simple, childlike faith is replaced with smart, business-oriented brains. Change becomes nearly impossible because the ball and chain of bureaucracy is too strong.

This shift has happened to some of the finest movements in the history of the Church. Even right now there are some that are going through a terrible crisis. And we should not think that, regardless of the organization with which we serve, we are immune to this change. It can happen to us!

Keep in mind—I am not saying that structure is wrong. With the growth of any movement, structure is vital, for you cannot function without discipline. The last verse of the book of Judges says, "In those days there was no king in Israel; everyone did what was right in his own eyes" (Judges 21:25). The next verse in the Bible is Ruth 1:1, which says, ". . . there was a famine in the land." No army can survive without discipline. No nation can survive without discipline. And no organization can survive without discipline.

But what I am talking about is the heart. The danger we must avoid is not discipline and structure, but replacing love, enthusiasm, freedom and empowerment with laws, regulations and power-based structures. When that happens, do you know who pays for it? The lost world . . . and our children who are growing up within the context of our ministries.

Transformational Becomes Transactional

This is when the motivation changes from one of heart condition to one of external rewards and benefits. Instead of, "I am so excited to be here; God is fresh and real, and our family is growing in His grace," the attitude is more like, "What do I get out of it—money, position, recognition?" As time goes by in an organization, people start thinking more about benefits and vacation time than service from a sold-out heart.

When believers in the book of Acts were beaten up and persecuted, the Bible says that they regarded it as a privilege that they were considered worthy to suffer for Jesus' name (see Acts 5:41). Paul tells us in Philippians 1:29 that "it has been granted [to us] . . . to suffer for His sake," or in other words, our "gift to suffer." Tradition says that when Peter was eventually sentenced to die by crucifixion, he asked to be crucified head down, as he did not feel worthy to die in the same manner as his Lord. For those who sold all to receive the precious pearl of great price, nothing could hold them back. They wouldn't ask, "What can I get out of it?" but rather, "What can I give?"

But as time passed, things began to change in the first-century church as well. Paul writes in Philippians 2:21, "All seek their own."

And what about you—where do you stand in this chronology? Are you feeling that the burden is too heavy for you? Do you wonder, "How long can I keep doing this? It's too hard to keep going. I don't know why I am do-ing it anymore. What about the future? Is all this worth doing?" Somehow, very privately, deep within your heart, these questions and thoughts can begin to burn and grow, even while outwardly you appear to be full of enthusiasm and praise to God.

I am not saying in any way that we should not have a plan for vacation time, insurance benefits or any of these things. The danger lies, though, in our hearts going after these externals or after some kind of promotion or recognition. When that happens, the joy that used to fill your heart will fade away, and all that will be left is self-centered motivation.

Relational Becomes Rational

Back in the mid-80s, when God led one young man to join us and help with our computer, I remember the one question I asked him before we accepted him: "Are you willing to clean the toilets and wash the dishes for the rest of your life, and never touch another computer again?" You see, I wanted to know if he was willing to become a servant—that's all I wanted. When I heard that he was willing to do anything, then I was glad to have him join us.

I tell you this to make a point. My concern was not so much about whether or not he had a big degree or his expertise and skill in his area. I was looking for someone with a servant heart.

When an organization goes from relational to rational, its values change. Skill and competency become more important than allowing the Lord to work through people. Things are perceived rationally and logically rather than based on faith that will produce miracles.

But when God calls people to serve Him, He will look beyond the 99, who have the best brains but are not broken, to the 1 who is perhaps not as smart but who is humble and willing to be used. Paul says that God chose the foolish things of this world—the least and last, the nobodies—to confound the wise (1 Corinthians 1:27). That is His way. Paul tells us that he himself was gifted with a brilliant mind, a stellar education, an impeccable pedigree—but he valued knowing Christ above it all so he threw it away and regarded it as dung (Philippians 3:4–8, KJV).

What matters to God? Servanthood, brokenness and faithfulness. Look at Joseph's life. How much education and training did he have to become prime minister? I don't think he had ever been to school. How about Daniel—what type of preparation did he have to become one of the top rulers of Babylon? And what was Amos's job that led him to become a prophet of the living God? David's qualifications to become the mightiest king of Israel included sheep herding and being a refugee. These are not fairy tales. This is reality. This is the way God works.

Do I place a premium on ignorance, on people who have no ideas or education? No, that is not my point. What I am saying to you is that when an organization comes to the place where passion is no longer a central value and, instead, titles, recognition and degrees hold priority, it will go astray.

So what must be done in a situation like this? How can we walk carefully so that we can avoid these three pitfalls? Let us explore that in the next chapter.

CHAPTER THREE

What Must We Do?

———◆———

Karl Marx said, "Philosophers have only interpreted the world differently. The point is to change it."[1] You can have all the ideas, dreams and desires for change in the world, but that will not make one ounce of change.

So, how do I effect change in the people around me—or in an entire society? It has to do with a deliberate decision on my part, as an individual, to change. Thinking about change only produces new philosophies, as Marx observed; it is only changed people who will see progress in others' lives around them.

If we stray away, how do we recover God's

original plan for us? How do we change? What must we do?

Abandonment

If our radical lives have become conventional, the way out is to start over. If we have come to the place at which we have accepted the means to the end as the end in itself, it is time for us to leave that all behind. Begin to work with the end in mind. We should no longer ask *how* we are going to get things done. That will automatically be answered if we concentrate on what we must do to change and move forward.

We must pray for the Holy Spirit to give us a fresh vision of hell, of the lost world and of revival. Abandonment means going back to the original vision and passion for which the Lord called us (Revelation 2:4–5). It means we are no longer motivated to serve because of structure or because of a leader who is over us; now we are gripped with the vision we have received.

Abandonment always causes people to become more innovative at what they do. They take ownership of the tasks they've been given. They now have freedom to make decisions—and the mistakes that naturally accompany those decisions.

In no way am I saying that we should

abandon structure altogether. A train can't run without its rails, and neither can an organization move forward without structure and leadership. But if there is no fire, no steam, no fuel, the train will go nowhere. What we must do is pray that God will protect us from stagnancy and a conventional life; and we must be willing to abandon whatever is holding us back from the radical edge (Philippians 3:13–15).

Decontrol

If you have raised or are raising children, you are aware of the delicate balance there is between freedom and accountability. As they grow physically, you slowly allow them to grow in areas of taking responsibility and making their own decisions.

As Jesus was leaving the disciples to return to heaven, He did not present them with a carefully planned agenda and schedule for world evangelism. Instead, what Jesus gave them was a passion and a vision that drove them to the ends of the earth and filled them with a willingness to lay down their lives for His sake. They never walked away from their calling, because they were following Jesus out of love and freedom.

That same balance between accountability and freedom must exist in an organization.

When Jacob worked 14 long, hard years of anguish to win Rachel's hand in marriage, the Scripture says it was like a few days because of his love for her (Genesis 29:20). No one forced him into it. He simply loved her. In the same way, within the context of accountability and submission to spiritual authority, we must have freedom to serve our Lord with love and joy, not because of some demands that are made of us.

My philosophy has always been that if the Lord called someone, then I will see the fruit of that calling in their confession, their circumstances, their maturity, their faithfulness and their trustworthiness. I don't ever want to come to a place where I demand respect and hold a heavy hand over my brothers and sisters.

Let us not end up with a life filled with heaviness, control and calculation. If an individual has been entrusted with a particular responsibility within the ministry, let us regard him as our leader with regard to *that* responsibility. Let us give each other freedom to make mistakes, and then we will grow as an organization. If we don't, we will die from within.

Empowerment

What do we do when our relationship-oriented ministry has become more focused on ability rather than servanthood? We must come to the place at which we let go of our controls and give freedom to one another. Empowerment happens when we can say to a brother or sister, "By the grace of God, I just want to trust you. Do the best you can—dream the best you can—and let us continue moving forward."

Empowerment happens when we give freedom to faith and potential in our dealings with people. Those who are in a position of responsibility over others should be discipling at least one person to take their place (2 Timothy 2:2).

I believe that the best is yet to come. Nearly 3 billion people are waiting to hear the Gospel; the Lord has committed this burden to the Body of Christ and will continue to work in us. We have the opportunity to change our generation! And I believe that the Lord will continue to bless the Church with growth to accomplish His task—through many means such as increasing staff, expanding physical facilities and raising needed finances.

One of the greatest blessings God raises up within an organization is the leadership. The responsibility for a ministry rests not upon one man, but upon a group of leaders. I am committed to the leaders in our organization, so much so that if their consensus is different than my own plan, I am willing to change. I have no desire to have my own way in anything.

No matter how the size of an organization increases, it is important to continue to maintain unique love, fellowship and excitement about what the organization does. Let us continue to develop a culture within our organizations in which individuals have the freedom to do their best and grow personally, without compulsion, restrictions, rules or regulations; but with the perspective of submission and reasonable structure. Let us keep the freedom the Lord has given us and never lose the original vision He has set before us.

There is a balance that is absolutely important when it comes to freedom. Consider this example:

A bird has two wings, and can only fly straight if both wings are healthy, functioning normally and operating simultaneously.

Likewise, as people grow together in any ministry, there are two "wings" that must function simultaneously. One is the whole concept of continually renewing and maintaining freedom and freshness, both individually and as a ministry. The other "wing" is the framework of accountability and submission to leadership.

Both are absolutely vital if we are to continue moving forward, and both must function if we are to be equipped to do the work the Lord has given us. It is within this context of freedom and accountability that trust and empowerment work best.

You need to have the freedom to take ownership of your God-given responsibilities. So, as you look at the specific tasks that He has set before you in your ministry, take the freedom to pray, dream and imagine what He can do through you to reach the lost world!

We will discuss some very practical ways to implement these three steps in the next chapter.

CHAPTER FOUR

Practical Steps toward Restoration

———◆———

The simplest way to bring about change, as I mentioned in Chapter 3, is to start with *yourself*. If I demand or expect change from others but refuse to do so myself, I will never see any difference. I must take the initiative and lead by my example. This works in a family, in an organization and in a society.

Let us take a look at some practical, "hands-on" ways through which we can maintain and renew the freshness and life within the ministry where we serve.

Radical Living Restored through Abandonment

Genuine revival comes from a personal, intimate encounter with the living God, not with the rules and regulations of an organization. How can I be a servant? When I know the One who is a servant of all. How can I be broken? When I meet with the One who was broken for the world. To be radical means you must be inwardly motivated.

Take time to think deeply, to pray sincerely and ask the Lord to renew, within your own heart, the vision of your ministry. Translate that vision into your specific area within the ministry. Search for unique ways that you can share and spread this vision within your own personal sphere of influence—your supporters and supporting churches, members of your local church, even believers you meet through your everyday activities. One longtime, faithful volunteer at our ministry originally started serving here because of her contact with a staff member in the laundry room of their apartment complex. The possibilities are virtually unlimited, but you can only access them when you have allowed the Lord to do the work in your heart.

Regularly review your mission statement[†], your vision[††] and your core values[†††]. Talk with leaders and others who have been with your ministry a while to learn what it was like in the early days.

To be radical, you must deliberately choose to do things that would help develop and cultivate your heart. It will not happen on its own. Take stock of your spiritual condition; face yourself honestly. Take responsibility for your own spiritual growth—don't shift the blame to others or to circumstances for your failures, shortcomings or stagnancy.

Transformational Living Restored through Decontrol

Think of all the people within your church or organization with whom you have influence—large or small, directly or indirectly. It may be an "official" position in which you have responsibility over them, or it may simply be that you share a bond because you live nearby, share similar tastes or have children who play together. Whatever the case, you can begin to think about those people: their potential, their giftings, their back grounds, their testimonies, their character and their dreams.

---

† A mission statement outlines the direction for your life or organization—the compass that keeps you going in the right direction.

†† The vision fulfills the mission statement with the actual steps—the map you use to get to your destination.

††† The core values are the principles and standards with which you fulfill your mission statement.

As you begin to do so, you will find within yourself a growing appreciation for each one of their lives. Begin to pray specifically for each individual.

The life of Jesus, in its finest manifestation, was all about caring for others. "The Son of Man did not come to be served, but to serve" (Mark 10:45). Let us be continually thinking of how we can bless and encourage others. Those who are in responsible positions within the organization need to be considering how to continually build up and "recharge" those who are under their authority and how to develop each one based on his or her abilities and giftings. What matters is not so much money, housing or things. People matter most.

Motivate others, not through power and heavy-handed techniques or through benefits, false hopes or manipulations but through love, grace, encouragement, approval, forgiveness, correction, challenge and integrity—and in some cases prayer and fasting. Do what it takes, as the Lord gives you the grace, to work toward really becoming one. We are not one just because we work together—it is because we genuinely care for one another.

I can testify that nearly every miracle that happened in our ministry came about not just as a result of my efforts or prayers, but also because a few individuals prayed, fasted, believed and stuck together. It had nothing to do with position or power. God's only method for getting things done, moving His kingdom forward and doing miracles *is* men and women. The work comes only secondary to the people who do the work.

Relational Living Restored through Empowerment

When you have influence over someone, whether it is a position of authority or simply the advantage of experience through having served a longer period of time in your ministry, you should never use that influence to get things done or make things happen. Force, veiled threats or intimidation, even when spiritually disguised, are never a substitute for love, mercy and grace.

Make sure that you place a higher value, above anything else, on a person's inner reality, character, humility, and brokenness and on a heart that seeks no glory or ambition. Acts 6 tells how the Lord directed the apostles to select men for service.

Ask the Lord to show you a handful of people within that circle of influence, one or two perhaps, in whom you can invest your life and share your vision. If you have responsibility over them at the office, begin to train them to do your job. Be open and honest with them, even at the risk of rejection or unresponsiveness.

I would highly recommend that you regularly read—perhaps every three months or so—Gayle Erwin's *The Jesus Style*[1] and study through the book *Humility*[2] by Andrew Murray.

The disciples stuck with Jesus for no other reason than love. And it is crucial that we understand this as we relate to one another.

Conclusion

———◆———

Perhaps, as you've read through this booklet, you can identify with what I've shared. You recall the vibrancy and passion you shared with your fellow workers to reach the lost. You remember your enthusiasm to serve one another, the love and family atmosphere you enjoyed and the unity you experienced. But all those blessings you once enjoyed are now just a memory.

Is there hope for your church, your organization? Absolutely. You can return to the original vision of your ministry. You can once again experience life and joy between you and your coworkers.

I encourage you to determine in your heart to seek the Lord and listen for His voice. It is His life that will restore your ministry. It is His vision that will guide and direct you.

If this booklet has been a blessing to you, I would really like to hear from you. You may write to Gospel for Asia, 1800 Golden Trail Court, Carrollton, TX 75010.
Or send an email to kp@gfa.org.

Notes

Chapter 1

[1] Gayle Erwin, *The Jesus Style* (Cathedral City, CA: YAHSHUA Publishing, 1997), pp. 24–26.

Chapter 3

[1] Charles R. Swindoll, *The Tale of the Tardy Oxcart and 1,501 Other Stories* (Nashville, TN: W Publishing Group, 1988), p. 622.

Chapter 4

[1] Erwin, *The Jesus Style*.

[2] Andrew Murray, *Humility* (New Kensington, PA: Whitaker House, 1982).

Booklets by K.P. Yohannan

A Life of Balance
Remember learning how to ride a bike? It was all a matter of balance. The same is true for our lives. Learn how to develop that balance, which will keep your life and ministry healthy and honoring God. (80 pages)

Dependence upon the Lord
Don't build in vain. Learn how to daily depend upon the Lord—whether in the impossible or the possible—and see your life bear lasting fruit. (48 pages)

Discouragement: Reasons and Answers
Ready to defeat discouragement and move on? It can be done! Discover the reasons for discouragement, and find hope and strength for an overcoming life. (56 pages)

Journey with Jesus
Take this invitation to walk the roads of life intimately with the Lord Jesus. Stand with the disciples and learn from Jesus' example of love, humility, power and surrender. (56 pages)

Learning to Pray
Whether you realize it or not, your prayers change things. Be hindered no longer as K.P. Yohannan shares how you can grow in your daily prayer life. See for yourself how God still does the impossible through prayer. (64 pages)

Living by Faith, Not by Sight
The promises of God are still true today: *"Anything is possible to him who believes!"* This balanced teaching will remind you of the power of God and encourage you to step out in childlike faith. (56 pages)

Principles in Maintaining a Godly Organization
Remember the "good old days" in your ministry? This booklet provides a biblical basis for maintaining that vibrancy and commitment that accompany any new move of God. (48 pages)

Seeing Him
Do you often live just day-to-day, going through the routine
of life? We so easily lose sight of Him who is our everything.
Through this booklet, let the Lord Jesus restore your heart and
eyes to see Him again. (48 pages)

Stay Encouraged
How are you doing? Discouragement can sneak in quickly and
subtly, through even the smallest things. Learn how to stay
encouraged in every season of life, no matter what the circumstances may be. (56 pages)

That They All May Be One
In this booklet, K.P. Yohannan opens up his heart and shares
from past struggles and real-life examples on how to maintain
unity with those in our lives. A must read! (56 pages)

The Beauty of Christ through Brokenness
We were made in the image of Christ that we may reflect all
that He is to the hurting world around us. Rise above the things
that hinder you from doing this, and see how your life can
display His beauty, power and love. (72 pages)

The Lord's Work Done in the Lord's Way
Tired? Burned out? Weary? The Lord's work done in His way
will never destroy you. Learn what it means to minister unto
Him and keep the holy love for Him burning strong even in the
midst of intense ministry. A must-read for every believer!
(72 pages)

The Way of True Blessing
What does God value most? Find out in this booklet as K.P.
Yohannan reveals truths from the life of Abraham, an ordinary
man who became the friend of God. (56 pages)

When We Have Failed—What Next?
The best is yet to come. Do you find that hard to believe? If
failure has clouded your vision to see God's redemptive power,
this booklet is for you. God's ability to work out His best plan
for your life remains. Believe it. (88 pages)

Order booklets through:
Gospel for Asia, 1800 Golden Trail Court, Carrollton, TX 75010
Toll free: 1-800-WIN-ASIA
Online: www.gfa.org